Piano Concertos Nos. 1 and 2
in Full Score

EDWARD MACDOWELL

Introduction by
Brian Mann
Vassar College

Dover Publications, Inc.
Mineola, New York

Bibliographical Note

This Dover edition, first published in 2003, is a new compilation of two works by
Edward MacDowell originally published separately by Breitkopf & Härtel, Leipzig
and New York: *Erstes Konzert für Pianoforte mit Orchester (A moll), Op. 15* (1911);
and *Zweites Konzert für das Pianoforte mit Begleitung des Orchesters (D moll), Op.
23* (1907; copyright 1890 by Edward MacDowell). The introductory note by Dr.
Brian Mann was prepared specially for this edition. Main headings as well as lists
of contents and instrumentation are newly added.

We are grateful to the Sibley Music Library, Eastman School of Music, New
York, and to The Susan Colgate Cleveland Library of Colby-Sawyer College, New
Hampshire, for making these rare scores available to us for republication.

International Standard Book Number: 0-486-42666-1

Manufactured in the United States of America
Dover Publications, Inc., 31 East 2nd Street, Mineola, N.Y. 11501

A NOTE ON THE CONCERTOS

Like so many promising American musicians in the second half of the nineteenth century, Edward MacDowell (1860–1908) travelled to Europe to complete his musical studies. Already a brilliant pianist at sixteen, he went first to Paris, accompanied by his mother. The next year—dissatisfied with instruction at the Conservatoire—he continued on to Germany, pursuing his studies in Stuttgart, Wiesbaden, and in Frankfurt, where he studied with Joachim Raff, an important mentor. He remained in Germany until 1888, apart from a brief trip to the United States in 1884 on the occasion of his marriage to Marian Nevins, one of his American students.

In Frankfurt in the spring of 1882, at the age of twenty-one, the composer began work on his first large-scale work, the Piano Concerto in A minor, Op. 15. Its genesis comes with a remarkable story, first told in Lawrence Gilman's biography of the composer. One Sunday morning, the young pianist was unexpectedly visited by Raff, whom he much revered.[1]

> . . . He abruptly asked me what I had been writing. I, scarcely realizing what I was saying, stammered out that I had a concerto. He walked out on the landing and turned back, telling me to bring it to him the next Sunday. In desperation, not having the remotest idea how I was to accomplish such a task, I worked like a beaver, evolving the music from some ideas upon which I had planned at some time to base a concerto. Sunday came, and I had only the first movement composed. I wrote him a note making some wretched excuse, and he put it off until the Sunday after. Something happened then, and he put it off two days more; by that time I had the concerto ready.

An extraordinary story—which might even be true! On 29 May, MacDowell wrote to his mother that he had recently played the concerto for Raff, who "was very much pleased and [who] told me I must go to Weimar and play it to Liszt who would recommend it."[2] By this time MacDowell was already known to Liszt, who had heard him play on more than one occasion and had read the manuscript of his *First Modern Suite* for piano solo. Indeed, Liszt had written to MacDowell on 13 April, informing him that he would place the *Suite* among the works to be played at the July meeting of the Allgemeine Deutscher Musikverein in Zurich. When MacDowell played the concerto for Liszt some time in early June, he was assisted by one of Liszt's young protégés, the brilliant Eugen d'Albert, who played the piano reduction of the orchestral part. Liszt was impressed with the piece, and happy to accept MacDowell's dedication of the work, as a letter of 22 February 1883 reveals.[3] The concerto was published in 1884 in a version for solo with orchestral reduction for second piano; the full score, which did not appear until 1911, embodies a number of minor revisions.[4]

The second and third movements were first performed by Adele Margulies on 31 March 1885 in New York's Steinway Hall, in a concert conducted by Frank van der Stucken.[5] The first complete performance of the work was heard in Boston on 3 April 1888, when Benjamin Whelpley played it in Chickering Hall with an orchestra conducted by Benjamin Johnson Lang. On 5 July of the same year Teresa Carreño (1853–1917)—the brilliant Venezuelan pianist and early advocate of MacDowell's music—played the concerto in Chicago, in a concert conducted by Theodore Thomas.[6] When Carreño moved to Germany the following year, she was quick to incorporate the work in her repertoire, playing it with the Berlin Philharmonic on 13 February 1890, and again in Dresden on 28 October. After these two performances, however, she turned her attention exclusively to MacDowell's Second Concerto in D Minor. It was then the composer's turn to perform the work—which he did on 18 and 19 November 1892 with the Boston Symphony Orchestra under the baton of Arthur Nikisch. He performed this concerto several more times, in 1894 and 1896, after which—rather like Carreño—he turned his attention to the Second Concerto.

A few details from the MacDowells' honeymoon in 1884 shed interesting light on the composer's muse at work. Immediately after their marriage in July of that year, Edward and Marian sailed for England. In London they attended performances of several Shakespeare plays, including *Hamlet, Much Ado about Nothing,* and *Othello.* The brilliant acting of Ellen Terry and Henry Irving made an indelible impression on the young composer, who responded almost immediately with an outburst of creative energy. A sketch book from late 1884 (now in the Library of Congress) shows MacDowell planning two works of three movements each—six tone poems in the form of character portraits of Shakespearean characters. Arranged in gendered pairs, Opus 22 was to include *Hamlet, Benedick,* and *Othello;* Opus 23 would be comprised of *Ophelia, Beatrice,* and *Desdemona.* This plan was eventually modified, and in the following year MacDowell published (as Op. 22) a pair of symphonic poems entitled *Hamlet* and *Ophelia. Benedick* survives only in manuscript, as a piano duet.[7]

When MacDowell turned his attention to composing a second piano concerto, he had the happy inspiration of transforming *Benedick* into the scherzo that serves as the concerto's sparkling middle movement. He went on to complete the work in 1886; in 1890 it was published as Op. 23, with an orchestral reduction for second piano; as with the First Concerto, the full score did not appear until much later, in 1907. An autograph copy of this score is preserved in the Vassar College Library (Special Collections); a preliminary short score is presently in the Library of Congress.[8]

One of the most accomplished and often performed American works of its time, the Concerto in D Minor had two formidable proponents: the composer and Teresa Carreño, to whom the music was dedicated. MacDowell premiered the work in New York on 5 March 1889, under the direction of Theodore Thomas, performing it again the following month in his adopted home of Boston. He continued to play the concerto both in the United States and abroad—most notably in Paris on 12 July 1889 as part of a concert devoted to American music, conducted by Frank van der Stucken. The composer last performed this work on 14 May 1903, in London, the year before the first signs appeared of his slow but inexorable decline into senility and early death.

It was Carreño, however, who contributed most to the work's continuing popularity, appearing in nearly forty performances between 31 May 1891—when she first performed the work in Berlin—and 26 November 1915, when she played it in Stockholm, apparently for the last time.[9] And yet her commitment to MacDowell's work succumbed on two occasions to the force of inner or outer pressures. In a remarkable instance of apparent professional jealousy, Eugen d'Albert, to whom Carreño was briefly married, effectively forbade her from performing MacDowell's music. Her abandonment of MacDowell's music during these years led in turn to ill feeling between Carreño and the composer (and, more importantly, between Teresa and the composer's mother, Frances, a close friend of many years and a fierce advocate of her son's music).

It was not until the 1897–1898 season that Carreño once again took up MacDowell's cause, playing the Second Concerto in Cassel, Berlin, Wiesbaden and Stuttgart, then in Chicago and Boston the following year. After two more performances in 1900, in Leipzig and London, she set the work aside until November 1905. Personal feelings may have intruded here: in September 1901 both Frances and Marian MacDowell wrote disapprovingly to Carreño upon learning of her intention to marry for a fourth time.[10] Further letters touched on various slights, both real and imagined. Carreño, however, took up the work once again, now perhaps in response to MacDowell's tragic illness, for we know that she wrote to his mother expressing her sympathy for this grievous blow.[11] Between 1905 and 1915, she played the concerto more than twenty times, including performances on tour with the Boston Symphony during MacDowell's final days in January 1908, and, in a final gesture of friendship, at Carnegie Hall's MacDowell Memorial Concert, on 31 March 1908.

BRIAN MANN
Vassar College
Fall 2002

A graduate of the University of Edinburgh, Brian Mann holds M.A. and Ph.D. degrees in historical musicology from the University of California, Berkeley. A specialist in the 16th- and 17th-century Italian madrigal, Dr. Mann has more recently written about the life and works of Teresa Carreño. He teaches at Vassar College, Poughkeepsie, NY.

END NOTES

[1]The quote is taken from Lawrence Gilman, *Edward MacDowell: A Study* (New York: John Lane, 1908) (reprint edition New York: Da Capo Press, 1969). See pp. 16–17.

[2]See Margery Lowens, "The New York Years of Edward MacDowell" (Ph. D. diss; University of Michigan, 1971), p. 19.

[3]For facsimiles of Liszt's letters to MacDowell of 13 April 1882 and 22 February 1883, see Gilman, op. cit., plates between pp. 18 and 19. In the letter of 1883, Liszt accepts MacDowell's proposed dedication with the laconic (and ungrammatical) statement: "Mit aufrichtigem Vergnügen und Dank empfangt die Widmung Ihrer Concert."

[4]These revisions are briefly alluded to by Oscar Sonneck in his *Catalogue of First Editions of Edward MacDowell (1861–1908)* (Washington: Government Printing Office, 1917); see p. 13.

[5]Information on early performances of the Piano Concerto in A Minor is taken from Lowens, op. cit., pp. 27 ff.

[6]The day following the concert, Carreño wrote an eloquent letter to Thomas, reprinted in Rose Fay Thomas, *Memoirs of Theodore Thomas* (New York: Moffat Yard and Company, 1911), p. 316. The letter is presently in the Newberry Library, Chicago.

[7]See *Benedick: A Sketch for the Scherzo from the Second Concerto for Pianforte* (New York: Edward MacDowell Association, 1947).

[8]For an account of Vassar's MacDowell holdings, see "The Carreño Collection at Vassar College," the author's article in *Notes: Quarterly Journal of the Music Library Association* 47 (1991): 1064-1082. The Carreño Collection also preserves a complete set of manuscript parts for the Concerto in D Minor; these help establish performance dates and venues.

[9]Carreño's advocacy of MacDowell is admirably documented in Laura Marina Pita Parra, "Presencia de la Obra de Edward MacDowell en el Repertorio de Teresa Carreño," Universidad Central de Venezuela, Facultad de Humanidades y Educacion, Escuela de Artes (1999).

[10]Two brief excerpts from unpublished letters must suffice. On 24 September 1901, Frances MacDowell wrote to Carreño: "Let me first say that I had hoped you would continue to the end of your life entirely your own mistress of your life as you are entire mistress of your piano . . . Frankly, I am sorry that you could not content yourself with this life which you have led since you separated from d'Albert" (letter in Special Collections, Vassar College). On 29 September, Marian MacDowell wrote to Carreño: "I will not attempt to hide from you that it is a very great surprise to me and in many ways your decision is incomprehensible to me . . . " (letter in Caracas; see Pita, op. cit., p. 95). In spite of such protests, Teresa married Arthur Tagliapietra, her second husband's younger brother, in June of the following year.

[11]A letter (now in Caracas; see Pita, op. cit., p. 103) from Frances MacDowell to Carreño, written on 4 October 1905, reads, in part "Thank you for your kind sympathetic note regarding the illness of our boy . . . I can only say that we are very anxious. His condition is serious and the doctors all agree that he has only a 'fighting chance' for recovery."

Piano Concerto No. 1
in A minor
Op. 15

INSTRUMENTATION

2 Flutes [Flauti, Fl.]
2 Oboes [Oboi, Ob.]
2 Clarinets in A [Clarinetti, Cl.]
2 Bassoons [Fagotti, Fg.]

4 Horns in F [Corni, Cor.]
2 Trumpets in F [Trombe, Tr.]

Timpani [Timpani, Timp.]

Piano Solo [Piano]

Violin I, II [Violino, Viol.]
Viola [Viola, Vla.]
Cello [Violoncello, Vcl.]
Bass [Contra-Basso, C.B.]

Piano Concerto No. 1
in A minor, Op. 15
(1882)

I.

II.

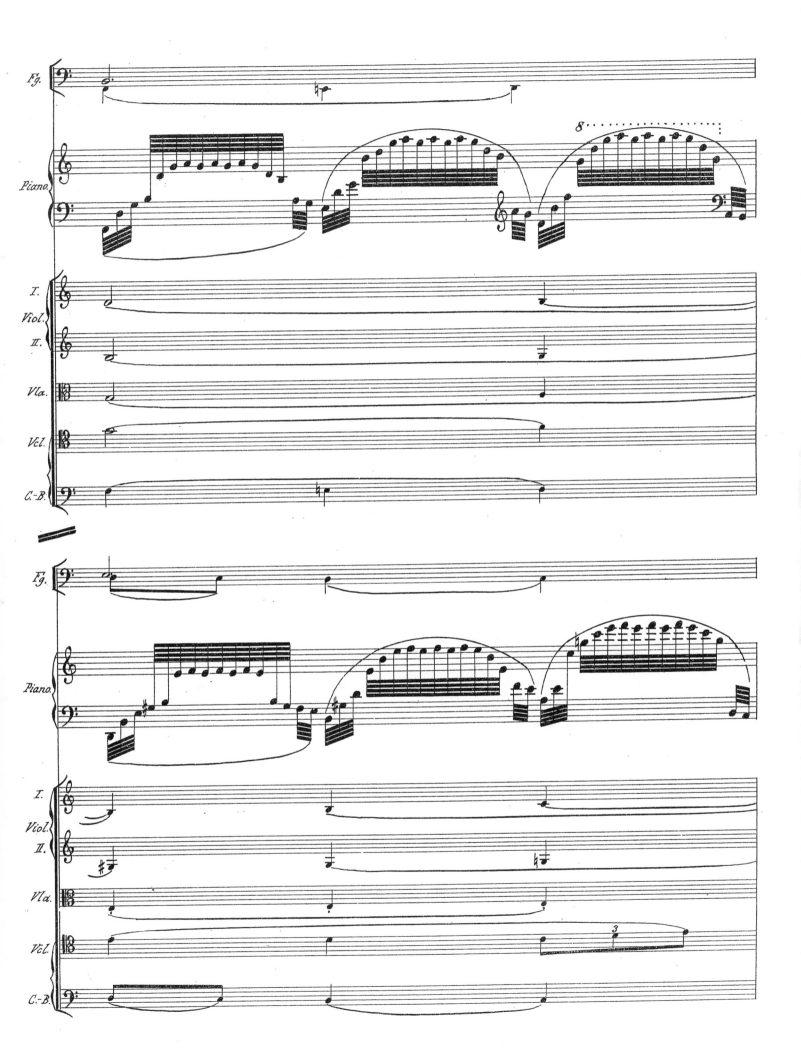

III.

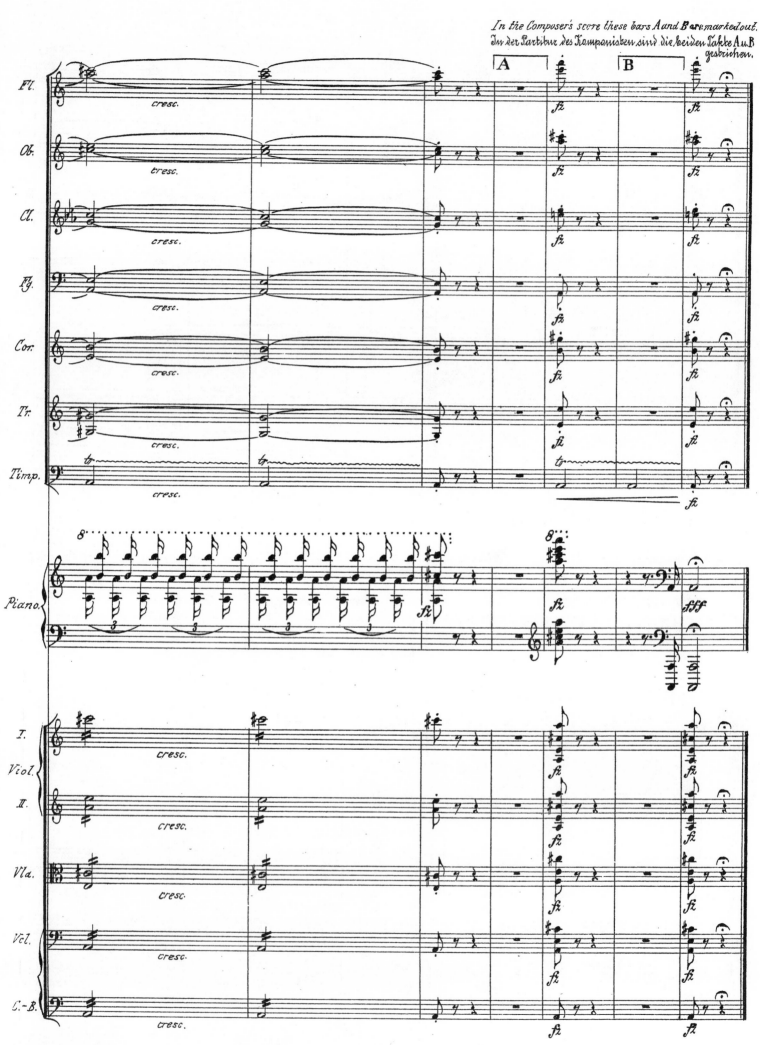

In the Composer's score these bars A and B are marked out.
In der Partitur des Komponisten sind die beiden Takte A u. B gestrichen.

Piano Concerto No. 2
in D minor
Op. 23

INSTRUMENTATION

2 Flutes [Flöten, Fl.]

2 Oboes [Hoboen, Hob.]

2 Clarinets in B♭ [Klarinetten, Klar. (B)]

2 Bassoons [Fagotte, Fag.]

4 Horns in F [Ventilhörner (Valve horns), Vent.-Hr.]

2 Trumpets in F [Ventiltrompeten (Valve Trumpets), Vent.-Tr.]

Timpani [Pauken, Pk.]

Piano Solo [Klavier]

Violin I [Erste Violinen, Viol.]

Violin II [Zweite Violinen, Viol.]

Violas [Bratschen, Br.]

Cellos [Violoncelle, Vcl.]

Basses [Kontrabässe, Kb.]

Piano Concerto No. 2
in D minor, Op. 23
(1884–6)

I.

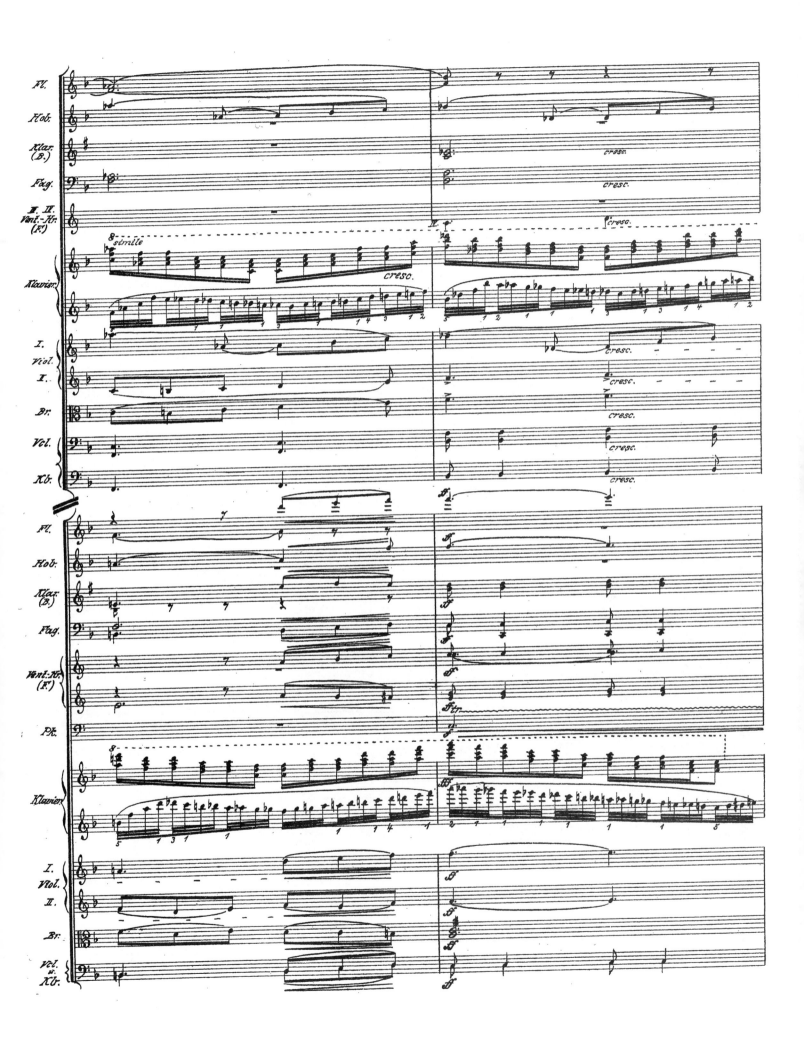

III.